BROADWAY SONGS

FOR HARMONICA

ARRANGED BY BOBBY JOE HOLMAN

ISBN 0-634-01670-9

7777 W. BLUEMOUND RD. P.O. BOX 13819 MILWAUKEE, WI 53213

BROADWAY SONGS
FOR HARMONICA

CONTENTS

How to Use the Music in This Book

This book is part of an ongoing series of themed publications covering a wide variety of musical styles. Each one provides a selection of the most popular and requested songs arranged for both the diatonic and chromatic harmonicas.

To understand the techniques required to play the songs presented, it is recommended that you thoroughly study both of my harmonica instruction books: The Hal Leonard Complete Harmonica Method—Book One—The Diatonic Harmonica, and The Hal Leonard Complete Harmonica Method—Book Two—The Chromatic Harmonica

Understanding this system will enable you to fully enjoy the musical treasures found within.

Heart to Harp,

Bobby Joe Holman

Understanding Harmonica Tablature for the Diatonic Harmonica

Before attempting to play the songs in this book, make sure you understand each harmonica tablature symbol, shown below. Understanding these symbols and reading the information on each song will enable you to learn and play these songs more easily and quickly.

To understand how to bend notes and which notes can be bent on a diatonic harmonica, refer to The Hal Leonard Complete Harmonica Method–Book One–The Diatonica Harmonica, Chapter 1. The diatonic harmonica, due to design limitations, requires this many symbols.

Blow

Draw

Half-step bend
(example: blow bend an E note down to an Eb/D♯)

Half-step bend
(example: draw bend an E note down to an Eb/D♯)

Whole-step bend
(example: blow bend a G note down to an F)

Whole-step bend
(example: draw bend a G note down to an F)

One and a half-step bend
(example: blow bend a C note down to an A)

One and a half-step bend
(example: draw bend a C note down to an A)

1 – 10   **Hole numbers on a diatonic harmonica**

A7   **Chord symbols for musical accompaniment**

Eb to C   **Change from one diatonic harmonica to another in a different key**

Ain't Misbehavin'
from AIN'T MISBEHAVIN'
Words by Andy Razaf
Music by Thomas "Fats" Waller and Harry Brooks

Key: Eb
Harmonica: Eb

Bali Ha'i
from SOUTH PACIFIC
Lyrics by Oscar Hammerstein II
Music by Richard Rodgers

Key: F
Harmonica: B♭

Blue Skies

from BETSY

Words and Music by Irving Berlin

Key: C
Harmonica: C

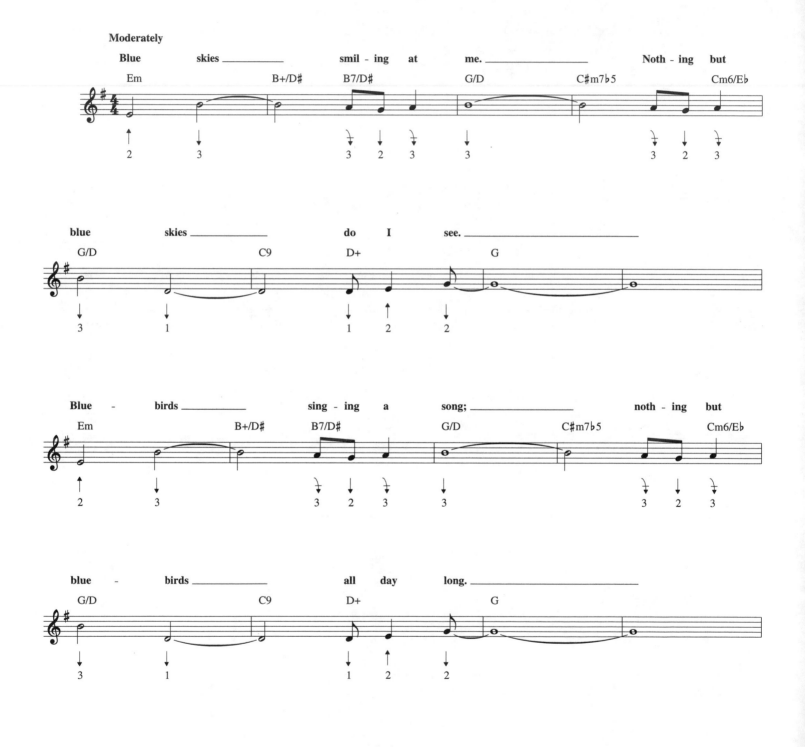

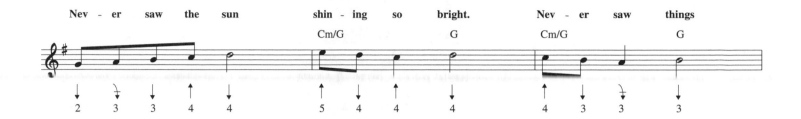

Nev - er saw the sun shin - ing so bright. Nev - er saw things

go - ing so right. No - tic - ing the days hur - ry - ing by; when you're in love,

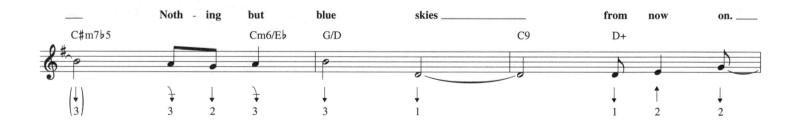

my how they fly. Blue days, _____ all of them gone. _____

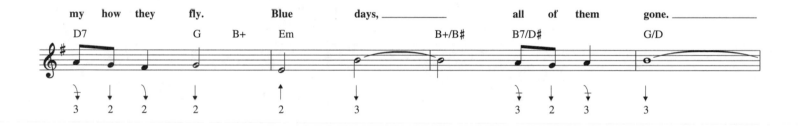

____ Noth - ing but blue skies _____ from now on. ____

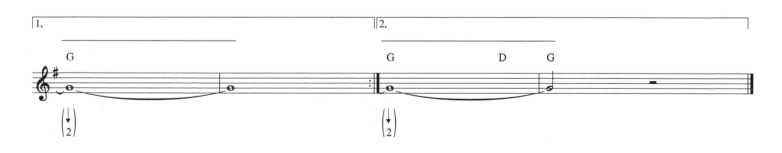

7

Camelot
from CAMELOT
Words by Alan Jay Lerner
Music by Frederick Loewe

Key: F
Harmonica: B♭

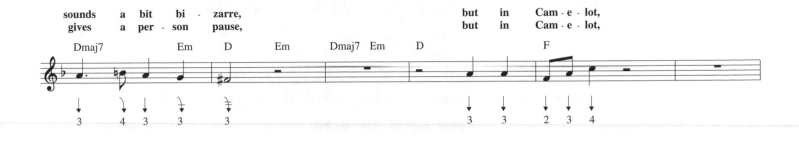

sounds a bit bi - zarre, but in Cam - e - lot,
gives a per - son pause, but in Cam - e - lot,

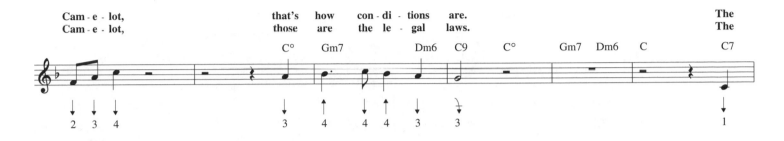

Cam - e - lot, that's how con - di - tions are. The
Cam - e - lot, those are the le - gal laws. The

rain may nev - er fall till af - ter sun - down. ____ By eight the morn - ing fog mus dis - ap -
snow may nev - er slush up - on the hill - side. ____ By nine P. M. the moon - light must ap -

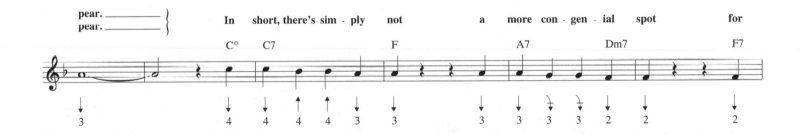

pear. _____ } In short, there's sim - ply not a more con - gen - ial spot for
pear. _____ }

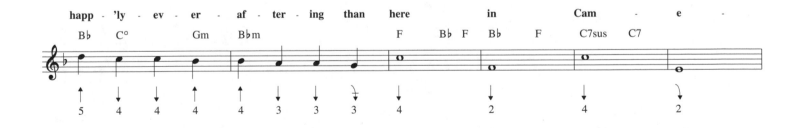

happ - 'ly - ev - er - af - ter - ing than here in Cam - e -

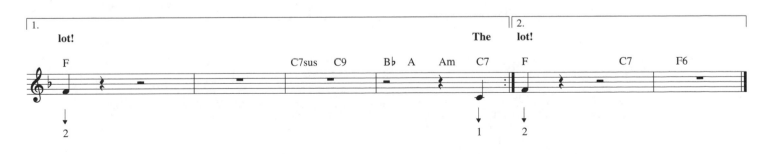

1.
lot! The
2.
lot!

9

Caravan
from SOPHISTICATED LADIES
Words and Music by Duke Ellington, Irving Mills and Juan Tizol

Key: A♭

Harmonica: D♭

Climb Ev'ry Mountain
from THE SOUND OF MUSIC
Lyrics by Oscar Hammerstein II
Music by Richard Rodgers

Key: C
Harmonica: C

Do-Re-Mi
from THE SOUND OF MUSIC
Lyrics by Oscar Hammerstein II
Music by Richard Rodgers

Key: C
Harmonica: C

Edelweiss
from THE SOUND OF MUSIC
Lyrics by Oscar Hammerstein II
Music by Richard Rodgers

Key: B♭
Harmonica: B♭

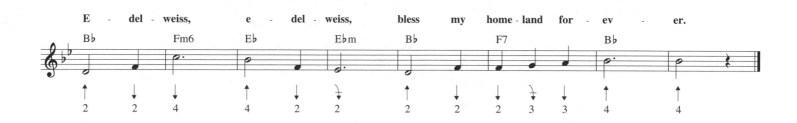

Gonna Build a Mountain
from the Musical Production STOP THE WORLD - I WANT TO GET OFF
Words and Music by Leslie Bricusse and Anthony Newley

Key: E♭
Harmonica: E♭, E, F

15

Give My Regards to Broadway

from LITTLE JOHNNY JONES
from YANKEE DOODLE DANDY

Words and Music by George M. Cohan

Key: B♭
Harmonica: B♭

Hello, Dolly!

from HELLO, DOLLY!

Music and Lyric by Jerry Herman

Key: Bb

Harmonica: Bb

Hello, Young Lovers
from THE KING AND I
Lyrics by Oscar Hammerstein II
Music by Richard Rodgers

Key: C
Harmonica: C

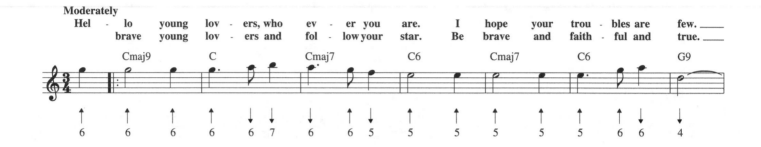

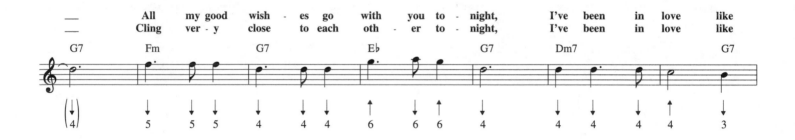

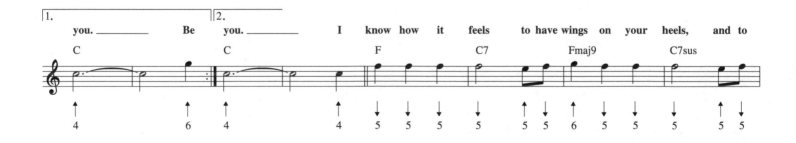

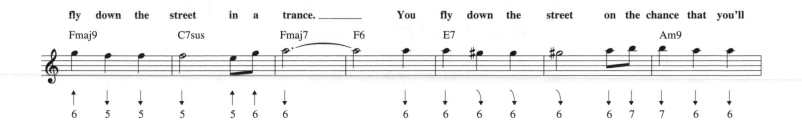

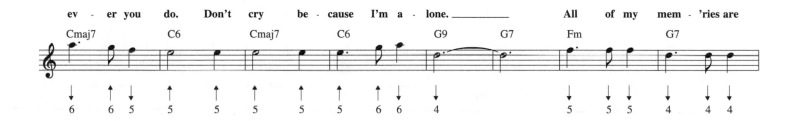

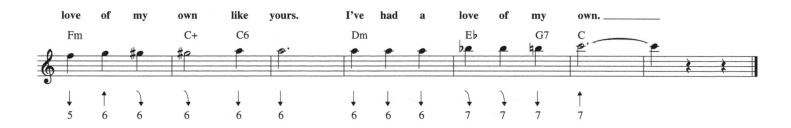

The Impossible Dream (The Quest)
from MAN OF LA MANCHA
Lyric by Joe Darion
Music by Mitch Leigh

Key: B♭
Harmonica: B♭

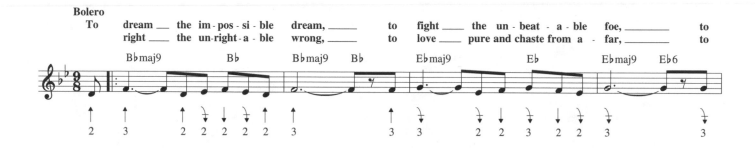

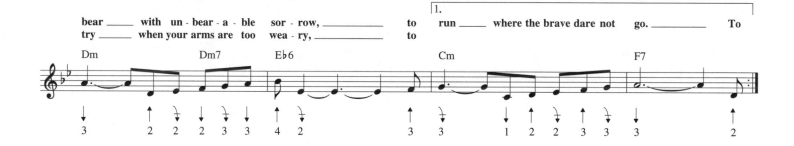

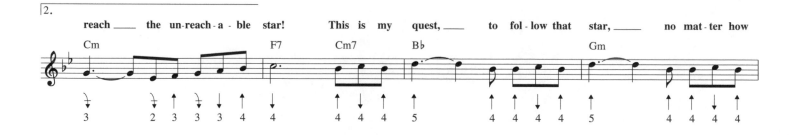

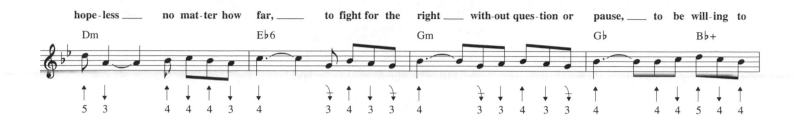

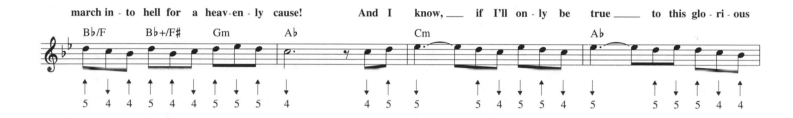

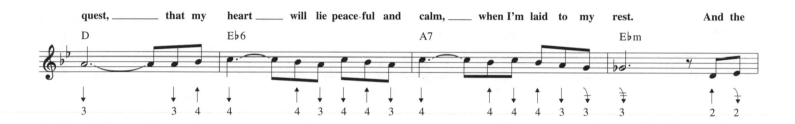

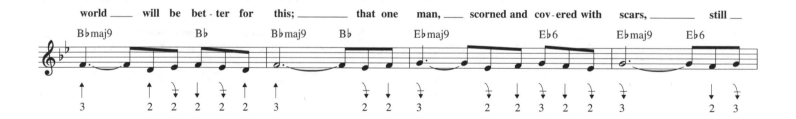

I've Grown Accustomed to Her Face
from MY FAIR LADY
Words by Alan Jay Lerner
Music by Frederick Loewe

Key: E♭
Harmonica: E♭

Masquerade

from THE PHANTOM OF THE OPERA

Music by Andrew Lloyd Webber
Lyrics by Charles Hart
Additional Lyrics by Richard Stilgoe

Key: C
Harmonica: C, Db, Eb

Memory
from CATS
Music by Andrew Lloyd Webber
Text by Trevor Nunn after T.S. Eliot

Key: C
Harmonica: C, A♭, E♭

Freely
Mid - night.___ Not a sound from the pave - ment.___ Has the moon lost her mem - 'ry?___ She is smil-ing a-

C ... Am ... F

7 7 7 7 8 7 6 7 7 7 7 8 7 6 6 6 5 6 6 6 5

lone. _____ In the lamp - light the with-ered leaves col - lect at my feet _____ and the

Em ... Dm7 ... Am7

5 5 6 6 4 5 5 6 6 7 7 7 6 6 5 4

wind _____ be - gins to moan. Mem - 'ry. ___ All a - lone in the moon - light ___ I can smile at the

G7 ... C ... Am

6 3 3 3 4 7 7 7 7 8 7 6 7 7 7 7 8 7 6

old days, ___ I was beau - ti - ful then. _____ I re - mem - ber ___ the time I knew what

F ... Em ... Dm7

6 6 5 6 6 6 5 5 5 6 6 4 5 5 6 6 7

Oklahoma

from OKLAHOMA!

Lyrics by Oscar Hammerstein II
Music by Richard Rodgers

Key: C
Harmonica: C

People
from FUNNY GIRL
Words by Bob Merrill
Music by Jule Styne

Key: B♭
Harmonica: B♭

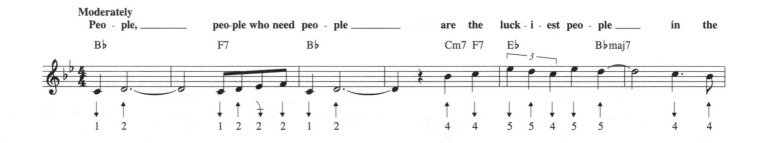

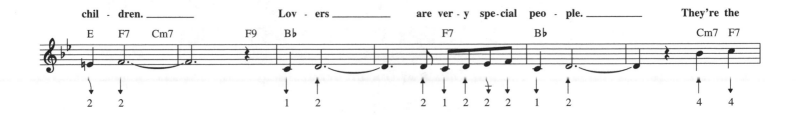

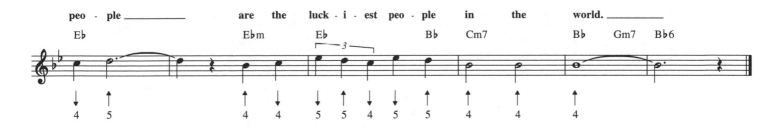

On a Clear Day (You Can See Forever)

from ON A CLEAR DAY YOU CAN SEE FOREVER

Words by Alan Jay Lerner
Music by Burton Lane

Key: G
Harmonica: G

Understanding Harmonica Tablature for the Chromatic Harmonica

Before attempting to play the songs in this section, the same approach is required to play these songs as in the diatonic section of this book. Make sure you understand each harmonica tablature symbol shown below to expedite the learning process.

Unlike the diatonic harmonica, the chromatic harmonica was designed to play every note in a two-octave scale (Hohner Chrometta #250), two and a half-octave scale (Hohner Chromatica #260), three-octave scale (Hohner Super Chromatica #270 or Chrometta #255) or four-octave scale (Hohner Super 64 #280). There are no bent notes required or changing of keys when playing this music on a chromatic harmonica.

To understand how to play this music on the chromatic harmonica, you should refer to The Hal Leonard Complete Harmonica Method – Book Two – The Chromatic Harmonica.

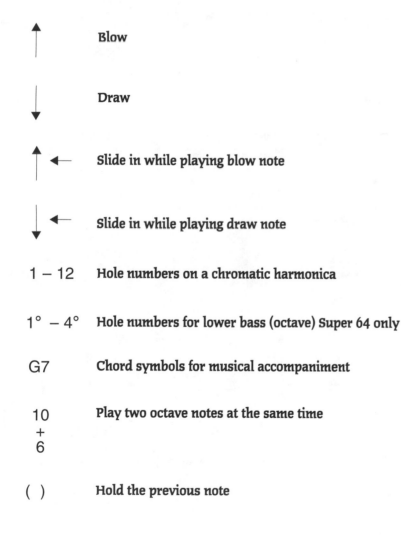

↑	Blow
↓	Draw
↑ ←	Slide in while playing blow note
↓ ←	Slide in while playing draw note
1 – 12	Hole numbers on a chromatic harmonica
1° – 4°	Hole numbers for lower bass (octave) Super 64 only
G7	Chord symbols for musical accompaniment
10 + 6	Play two octave notes at the same time
( )	Hold the previous note

Ain't Misbehavin'
from AIN'T MISBEHAVIN'
Words by Andy Razaf
Music by Thomas "Fats" Waller and Harry Brooks

Key: E♭
Harmonica: All chromatic harmonicas

Bali Ha'i
from SOUTH PACIFIC
Lyrics by Oscar Hammerstein II
Music by Richard Rodgers

Key: F
Harmonica: All chromatic harmonicas

Blue Skies
from BETSY
Words and Music by Irving Berlin

Key: C
Harmonica: All chromatic harmonicas

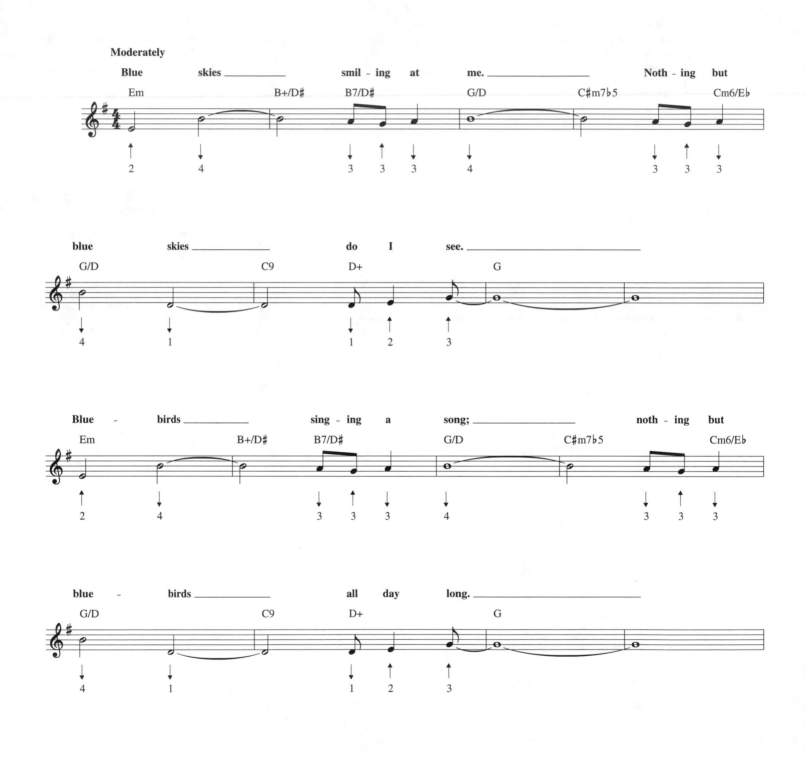

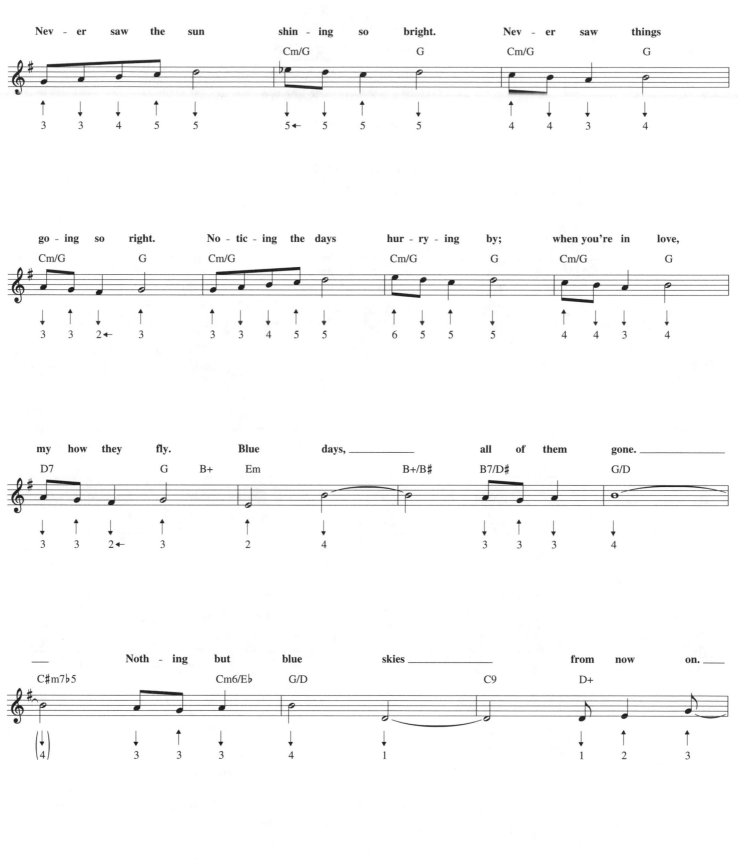

Camelot
from CAMELOT
Words by Alan Jay Lerner
Music by Frederick Loewe

Key: F
Harmonica: All chromatic harmonicas

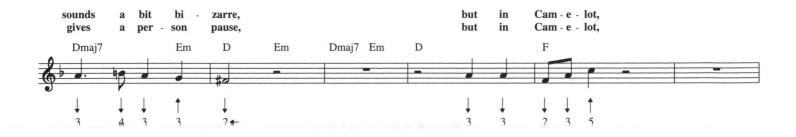

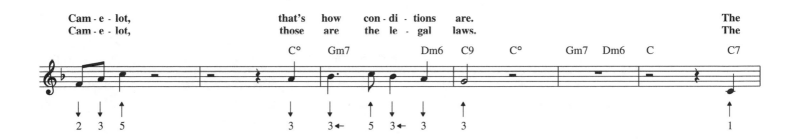

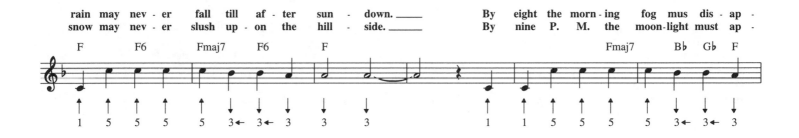

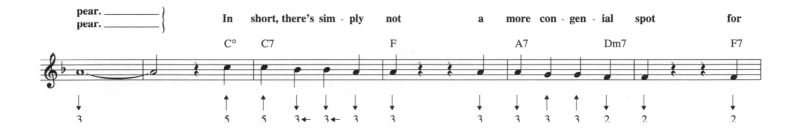

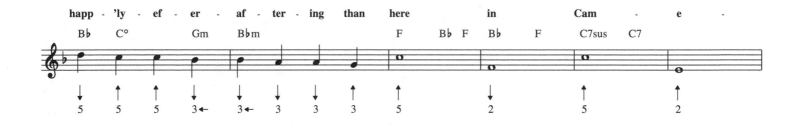

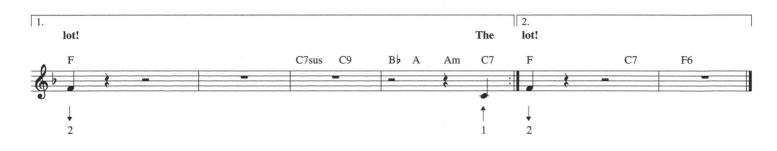

Caravan
from SOPHISTICATED LADIES
Words and Music by Duke Ellington, Irving Mills and Juan Tizol

Key: A♭
Harmonica: All chromatic harmonicas

Climb Ev'ry Mountain
from THE SOUND OF MUSIC
Lyrics by Oscar Hammerstein II
Music by Richard Rodgers

Key: C
Harmonica: All chromatic harmonicas

Do-Re-Mi
from THE SOUND OF MUSIC

Lyrics by Oscar Hammerstein II
Music by Richard Rodgers

Key: C
Harmonica: All chromatic harmonicas

Edelweiss
from THE SOUND OF MUSIC
Lyrics by Oscar Hammerstein II
Music by Richard Rodgers

Key: Bb
Harmonica: All chromatic harmonicas

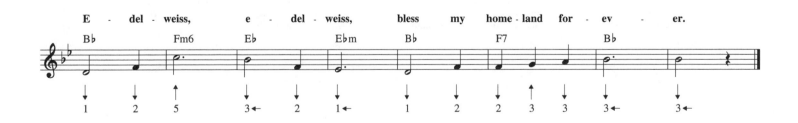

Gonna Build a Mountain

from the Musical Production STOP THE WORLD - I WANT TO GET OFF

Words and Music by Leslie Bricusse and Anthony Newley

Key: E♭

Harmonica: Hohner Super 64 only

Give My Regards to Broadway

from LITTLE JOHNNY JONES
from YANKEE DOODLE DANDY

Words and Music by George M. Cohan

Key: B♭
Harmonica: All chromatic harmonicas

Brightly

Give my re-gards to Broad-way. Re-mem-ber me to Her-ald Square. _____

B♭　Dm7 B♭ B♭° Cm7 E♭m6 F7　Cm7　F7 F+ B♭6 B° F7

↓ ↑ ↓ ↓ ↑ ↓ ↓ ↓ ↑ ↑ ↑ ↑ ↓ ↓ ↓
2 3 3 3← 5 3← 3 2 3 3 3 3 3 3 2

Tell all the gang at For-ty Sec-ond Street that I will soon be there. _____ Whis-per of

B♭ Dm7 B♭ B♭m6 F C7 F C#° Dm Gm Gm7 B♭m6 C6 C7 F7 E♭m6 F7 B♭ Dm7

↓ ↑ ↓ ↓ ↑ ↓ ↓ ↑ ↓ ↑ ↓ ↓ ↓ ↑ ↓ ↓ ↓ ↑ ↓
2 3 3 3← 3 3 3← 5 3 2 3← 3 3 3← 5 2 3 3

how I'm yearn-ing to min-gle with the old time throng. _____ Give my re-gards to

B♭ B♭° Cm7 E♭m6 F7 Cm7 F7 F+ B♭ B♭maj7 B♭7 G7 G+ G7

↓ ↑ ↓ ↓ ↑ ↑ ↑ ↓ ↓ ↓ ↓ ↑ ↓ ↓
3← 5 3← 3 2 3 3 3 3 3 2 5 4 3 5← 5

old Broad-way and say that I'll be there, ere long. long. _____

Cm G7 Cm7 G♭7 B♭ Gm C7 F7 B♭ B♭° Cm7 F7+5 B♭

|1. |2.

↑ ↓ ↑ ↓ ↑ ↓ ↓ ↓ ↑ ↓ ↓
5 4 5 3← 5 3← 5 3← 3← 5 3← 3←

Hello, Dolly!

from HELLO, DOLLY!

Music and Lyric by Jerry Herman

Key: Bb
Harmonica: Hohner Super 64 only

Hello, Young Lovers

from THE KING AND I

Lyrics by Oscar Hammerstein II
Music by Richard Rodgers

Key: F
Harmonica: Hohner Super 64 only

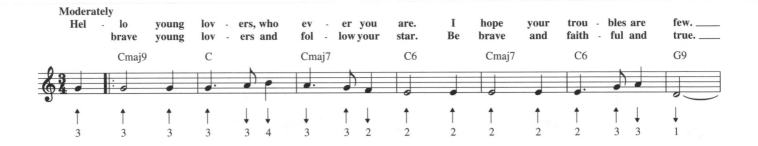

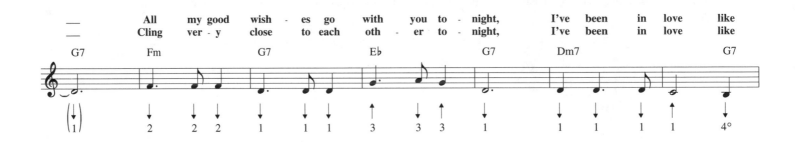

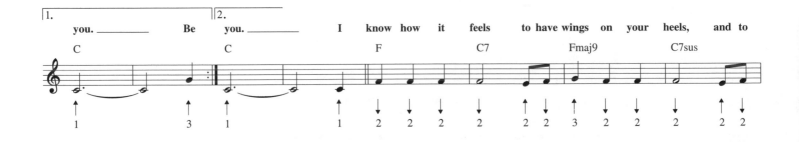

The Impossible Dream (The Quest)
from MAN OF LA MANCHA

Lyric by Joe Darion
Music by Mitch Leigh

Key: B♭
Harmonica: All chromatic harmonicas

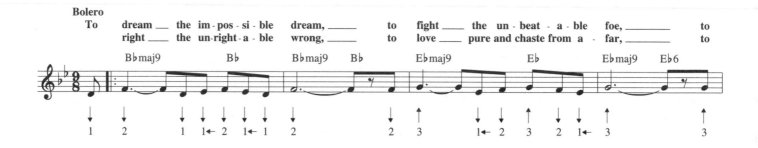

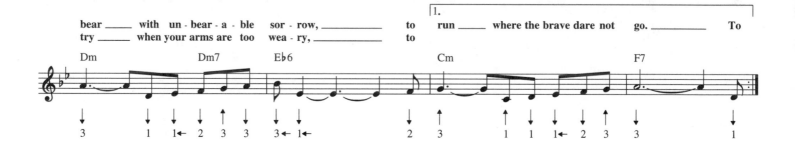

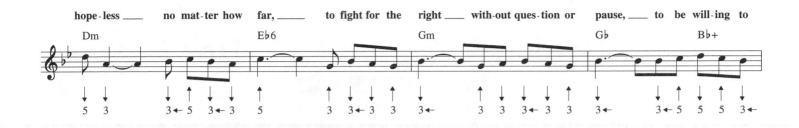

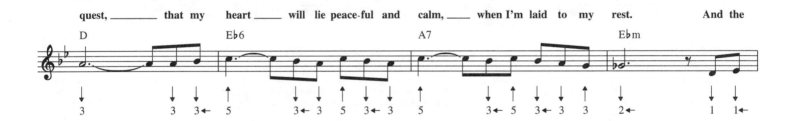

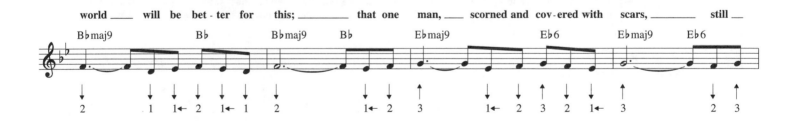

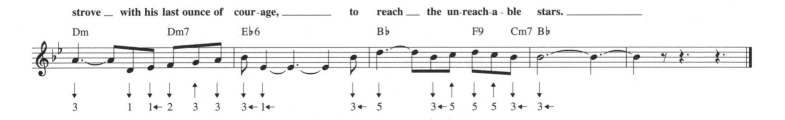

I've Grown Accustomed to Her Face

from MY FAIR LADY

Words by Alan Jay Lerner
Music by Frederick Loewe

Key: E♭
Harmonica: All chromatic harmonicas

Masquerade

from THE PHANTOM OF THE OPERA

Music by Andrew Lloyd Webber
Lyrics by Charles Hart
Additional Lyrics by Richard Stilgoe

Key: C
Harmonica: All chromatic harmonicas

Memory
from CATS
Music by Andrew Lloyd Webber
Text by Trevor Nunn after T.S. Eliot

Key: C
Harmonica: Hohner Super 64 only

Oklahoma
from OKLAHOMA!
Lyrics by Oscar Hammerstein II
Music by Richard Rodgers

Key: C
Harmonica: All chromatic harmonicas

People

from FUNNY GIRL

Words by Bob Merrill
Music by Jule Styne

Key: B♭
Harmonica: Hohner Super 64 only

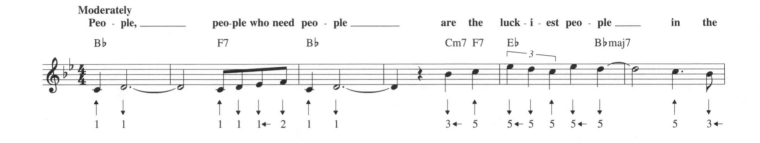

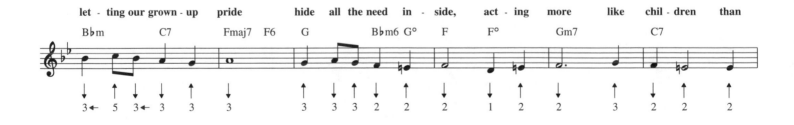

On a Clear Day (You Can See Forever)
from ON A CLEAR DAY YOU CAN SEE FOREVER

Words by Alan Jay Lerner
Music by Burton Lane

Key: G
Harmonica: Hohner Super 64 only

HAL LEONARD PRESENTS EIGHT GREAT HARMONICA BOOKS!

THE HAL LEONARD COMPLETE HARMONICA METHOD – THE DIATONIC HARMONICA
Bobby Joe Holman
The only harmonica method specific to the diatonic harmonica, covering all six positions. This book/CD pack contains 29 songs and musical examples that take beginners from the basics on through to the most advanced techniques available for the contemporary harmonica player. Each section contains appropriate songs and exercises (which are demonstrated on the CD) that enable the player to quickly learn the various concepts presented. Every aspect of this versatile musical instrument is explored and explained in easy-to-understand detail with illustrations. The musical styles include traditional, blues, pop and rock.
00841285 Book/CD Pack $12.95

THE HAL LEONARD COMPLETE HARMONICA METHOD – THE CHROMATIC HARMONICA
Bobby Joe Holman
The only harmonica method to present the chromatic harmonica in 14 scales and modes in all 12 keys! This book/CD pack will take beginners from the basics on through to the most advanced techniques available for the contemporary harmonica player. Each section contains appropriate songs and exercises (which are demonstrated on the CD) that enable the player to quickly learn the various concepts presented. Every aspect of this versatile musical instrument is explored and explained in easy-to-understand detail with illustrations. The musical styles include traditional, blues, pop and rock.
00841286 Book/CD Pack $12.95

BROADWAY SONGS
19 show-stopping Broadway tunes for the harmonica. Songs include: Ain't Misbehavin' • Bali Ha'i • Blue Skies • Camelot • Caravan • Climb Ev'ry Mountain • Do-Re-Mi • Edelweiss • Give My Regards to Broadway • Gonna Build a Mountain • Hello, Dolly! • Hello, Young Lovers • I've Grown Accustomed to Her Face • The Impossible Dream (The Quest) • Masquerade • Memory • Oklahoma • On a Clear Day (You Can See Forever) • People.
00820009 $8.95

CHRISTMAS CAROLS AND HYMNS
19 songs, including Auld Lang Syne • Deck the Hall • The First Noel • It Came Upon the Midnight Clear • Jingle Bells • Joy to the World • Silent Night • We Wish You a Merry Christmas • and more.
00820008 $8.95

CLASSICAL FAVORITES
18 classical treasures, including: By the Beautiful Blue Danube • Clair De Lune • The Flight of the Bumble Bee • Gypsy Rondo • Two-Part Invention in C Major • Lascia Ch'io Pianga • Minuet (from Don Giovanni) • Minuet in G Major, K. 1 • Piano Sonata No. 14 in C# Minor ("Moonlight") Op. 27 No. 2 First Movement Theme • Symphony No. 6 in F Major ("Pastoral") Third Movement • Prelude in G Minor Op. 23 No. 5 • Surprise Symphony • The Swan (Le Cygne) • Theme from Swan Lake • Symphony No. 5 in C Minor, First Movement Excerpt • Symphony No. 9 in D Op. 125 Second Movement Theme • Waltz in C# Minor • Waltz of the Flowers.
00820006 $7.95

MOVIE FAVORITES
19 songs from the silver screen. Includes: Alfie • Bless the Beasts and Children • Chim Chim Cher-ee • The Entertainer • Georgy Girl • Maybe This Time • Midnight Cowboy • Moon River • Theme from "Picnic" • Puttin' on the Ritz • (Ghost) Riders in the Sky (A Cowboy Legend) • Speak Softly, Love (Love Theme) • Stormy Weather (Keeps Rainin' All the Time) • Tenderly • A Time for Us (Love Theme) • Unchained Melody • What a Wonderful World • Zip-A-Dee-Doo-Dah.
00820014 $8.95

POP/ROCK FAVORITES
17 classic hits, including Abraham, Martin and John • All I Have to Do Is Dream • Blueberry Hill • Copacabana (At the Copa) • Daydream • Green Green Grass of Home • Hanky Panky • Happy Together • Oh, Pretty Woman • Runaway • Sixteen Candles • Sleepwalk • Something • Stand By Me • Tears on My Pillow • Tell It Like It Is • Yakety Yak.
00820013 $8.95

TV FAVORITES
More than 20 couch potato hits. Includes: The Ballad of Davy Crockett • Theme from "Beauty and the Beast" • Theme from "Bewitched" • The Brady Bunch • Brandenburg Concerto No. 2 • Bubbles in the Wine • Call to Glory • Danny Boy (Londonderry Air) • Father Knows Best Theme • Hands of Time • Happy Days • The Little House (On the Prairie) • Mariko Love Theme • Nadia's Theme • Theme from Ninth Symphony • The Odd Couple • Twin Peaks Theme • Theme from "The Untouchables" • Victory at Sea • William Tell Overture • Wings.
00820007 $8.95

0900

Prices, contents, and availability subject to change without notice.